GARDEN ORNAMENTS
& STATUARY

· GARDENING · BY · DESIGN ·

GARDEN ORNAMENTS
& STATUARY

· PETER · MCHOY ·

Ward Lock Limited · London

© Ward Lock Ltd 1987

First published in Great Britain in 1987
by Ward Lock Limited, 8 Clifford Street
London W1X 1RB, an Egmont Company

House editor Denis Ingram

Text set in Bembo Roman
by HBM Typesetting Limited, Chorley, Lancashire

Printed and bound in France by Brodard

British Library Cataloguing in Publication Data

McHoy, Peter
    Garden ornaments and statuary.
    1.   Garden ornaments and furniture
    I.   Title
    717   SB473.5

ISBN 0-7063-6550-X

CONTENTS

ACKNOWLEDGEMENTS

The publishers are grateful to the following persons and agencies for granting permission to reproduce the following colour photographs: Peter McHoy (pp. 10, 11, 58, 62, 70 & 71); Bob Challinor (pp. 19, 22, 23, 35, 50, 66 & 74); Impact Photos/Pamla Toler (p. 18); Hugh Palmer (pp. 27, 39, 63 & 75); Michael Boys (p. 31); Tessa Traeger (pp. 34, 47, 55); John Heseltine (pp. 3, 38, 42, 67). The photographs on pp. 15 & 43 were taken by Bob Challinor.

All the line drawings were drawn by Nils Solberg.

The designs of the sundials in Fig. 5 and of the armillary sphere in Fig. 6 are shown courtesy of Brookbrae Ltd.

PREFACE

Many gardeners associate statues and other garden ornaments with the large gardens of the past, as things to admire on garden visits, rather than to own and use creatively in their own smaller, modern gardens.

This book will hopefully dispel that image and show that they are as relevant in garden design today as they have ever been. Once you decide that your garden should have a strong *design*, as well as interesting plants, this becomes obvious as you have to think about shape and form, and focal points. Statues and ornaments can help you achieve all three.

This is a book about *good*, not expensive, taste. If you can afford expensive original antiques, or can commission a piece of sculpture specially for your garden, as often happened in the past, your garden will be the richer for it. But many ideas will cost you very little yet probably achieve as strong an impact. How and where you choose to use ornaments can be as important as what you use. An object that could look hideous in one part of the garden could look superb in the correct setting.

The photographs in this book reflect a wide range of settings, from famous gardens with valuable ornaments contemporary with the garden, to in-expensive mass-produced pieces in modern gardens.

Each enhances its particular site and provides year-round interest, though plants thrive and fade with the seasons. The pictures should help stimulate ideas of your own and hopefully enable you to visualize how your garden could be improved with a few well-chosen garden ornaments.

But don't dash out and buy something immediately because a particular idea has inspired you. Every garden – like every home – is different, so ornaments should reflect your own taste and personality. Above all they should fit in with the garden. If you buy something merely because it catches your eye, and then try to find somewhere to site it, it probably won't work. Part of the fun of using garden ornaments is to take time and savour the choosing and the buying, visualizing how each piece could look in a particular spot, or in association with certain plants. A statue or ornament will be one of the most permanent, unchanging features of your garden, so do take time to get it right!

Once you start using statues and ornaments in your own garden, you'll probably start to appreciate those in the gardens you visit. You'll look at their use as focal points, take in the kind of material they are made of, and appreciate their detail in a way you probably didn't before. In short, taking an interest in garden statuary and ornaments amounts to more than making a single purchase for your garden. It can enhance your appreciation of gardens and garden design in general.

Some gardeners make a point of bringing back an ornament of some kind from a holiday, usually something with local associations, even if only made by a local craftsman. You'll have to be careful not to make a 'gnome garden', though, and it takes skill to find spots where they will look right when you get them home, but some people manage it.

A final word of warning. You could end up completely redesigning your garden to show off your garden ornaments to best effect. If you do, you will have learned the lesson of good design.

Don't be put off by classical images or deterred by fear of cost; don't assume that your garden is too small, too large or too 'ordinary'; and don't let anyone lead you to believe that they have a monopoly of good taste. If you follow the principles suggested in this book, you won't go far wrong. Hopefully you will discover the pleasure and uses of garden ornaments . . . and learn to express yourself through your garden.

P.McH.

1

LOOKING BACK

If you find history boring, you can pass to the next chapter. You will then have missed an interesting part of the story of garden development, though you will still be able to get the best from the vast range of ornaments now available. However, understanding how ornaments were used during the evolution of the modern garden can be of real practical help. The setting and scale may be very different but many of the principles followed by past landscape architects remain valid today, even for small modern gardens. A glimpse at the development of garden ornaments will also help you better appreciate the great gardens that you visit.

The first statues or ornaments were probably idols or monuments to a deity, but the realization that they could enhance and decorate a garden probably came after the Romans conquered Greece and carried off many of their statues to decorate the gardens and palaces of Rome.

We have quite a clear picture of the way the Romans used statues and garden ornaments. The peace and prosperity that their conquests brought to Rome encouraged the development of gardens as we think of them today. There were, of course, famous gardens before this – the Hanging Gardens of Babylon are an obvious example – but we have some quite detailed descriptions of Roman gardens. We know from plans of the Portico of Livia, which Augustus created in the Greek style, that a portico surrounded a sunken lawn, and that statuary and fine works of art, Greek in spirit, embellished some of the shady retreats amid the flower beds and pergolas. Pliny the Younger, nephew of the elder Pliny, wrote at length about his garden, giving us a splendid insight into the gardens of that period. He says that in front of the portico 'is a sort of terrace, embellished with various figures and bounded with a box hedge', while 'here and there little obelisks rise'.

Long after ancient Rome had collapsed, the Medici family settled just outside the walls of Florence, and by the fourteenth century had become wealthy and famous. Cosimo de Medici was born into this now influential family in 1389. In later life he commissioned Michelozzo Michelozzi to replan his villa at Careggi along classical lines. The basic ideas of the Renaissance may have been formulated in this villa and garden. Some historians argue that they had already been evolving, but in the Careggi villa garden Renaissance ideas seem to have been well established.

Statues and ornaments weren't an important feature at first, and even as late as 1483 Poggio Bracciolino was

This corner of a small town garden shows how effective ornaments can be even in a small garden.

If you have a conservatory, a statue can add a touch of distinction and bring a dull corner to life.

laughed at by his friends for putting classical statues in his garden. But the wheel was turning and Lorenzo de Medici had started to collect statues for one of the gardens, where he displayed them for artists to study.

Statuary had its first real impact on Renaissance gardens when Pope Julius II, who had a famous collection of statues, decided to move them to the Vatican. He chose the Villa Belvedere for them, but it was a question of integrating them with the garden, and linking the garden with the Papal lodgings, separated by a belt of rising ground. He asked Donato Bramante, who had studied the ruins of ancient Rome, to take on the job . . . and so the principles of Renaissance gardening as we now know them were born. He made the architecture grow out of the site, related the garden to the axis of the house, and linked it with the landscape – a series of terraces gave the hillside architectural form. Symmetry and proportion were established, ornaments became an integral part of the garden, and their usefulness as focal points was realized.

Italian hill villas became home for many treasures, including some pieces found in the ruins of ancient Rome. The backdrop of cypress and box provided an ideal foil for marbles and other sculptures. The statuary gradually became more ornate and embellished, and water was sometimes used to bring them to life by playing over or through them. Many of the now classical forms such as balls, obelisks, pineapples and urns were developed.

We should bear in mind that the Italians probably made such good use of ornaments and water because they brought life and interest to gardens that lacked the range of colourful plants we have today. Orange and lemon trees, oleander, myrtle, box, bay, junipers, hollies, and cypress were probably the main plants they had available.

France followed the trend for statues and ornaments as integrated garden features when Charles VIII, after warring in Italy, saw how men of taste lived there. He set about trying to recreate a similar style in France. The French style gradually evolved, reaching a new height of glory with the gardens at the Palace of Versailles, which still stand as a monument to that period, with statuary used to emphasize the axial planning.

The gardens at Versailles were designed by Le Nôtre, who made extensive use of statues and fountains to punctuate important points around this vast garden. The influence of this great garden is still with us today even in quite small gardens – Versailles tubs and Versailles vases are still popular garden ornaments.

Although statues and ornaments were widely used in the great Renaissance gardens of Italy and France, they were often little more than incidentals in the overall design, and did not much influence the design itself. Yet many of these gardens would be very dull if stripped of their ornaments and sculptures – the terraces, clipped hedges, espaliered trees and massed shrubberies would soon lose much of their appeal. Even the water features would pale in significance without the sculptured fountains and masks.

By the mid-sixteenth century the influence of the Renaissance gardens had made an impact in England, and soon terraces were decorated with balustrading and statuary.

Many of the earliest ornaments specially sculptured for European gardens were mediaeval or Renaissance heraldic animals. Examples were to be found in the royal palace gardens in sixteenth-century England. Henry VIII brought a large number of Italian artists and workmen to England to embellish the Palace of Nonsuch and its gardens, for one still turned to Italy for the inspiration of garden ornament.

Not all early garden ornaments were purely decorative. Many were useful in origin. By the sixteenth century the fixed sundial had also become a free-standing ornament, and from the eighteenth century most sundials were set horizontally and supported on often decorative columns. The dials, made from copper, bronze or brass, were finely engraved. Well heads and cisterns also became decorative as well as functional features. Long after their practical application became obsolete with the progress of technology, sundials, well-heads, and lead water cisterns are used purely for their decorative effect.

Statuary really came into its own in England in the late seventeenth and early eighteenth centuries. Although classical in inspiration, there was a much greater blending of plants and water, composed rather like a picture. The Renaissance gardens used statues and urns worked from marble and stone, but by the end of the seventeenth century good sculptors could not keep up with the demand. This had to be met by figures and urns cast in lead.

The classical discipline gradually gave way to the pressures of the nineteenth century when mass-produced ornaments began to appear. Cast iron was used and various forms of artificial stone were already in use. A successful and cheaper alternative to stone, known as Coade ware (made by a firm called Coade & Seely) became popular in Britain by the early nineteenth century. It was actually more weather resistant than some quarried stones and was used for a range of architectural mouldings. Unfortunately the formula is no longer known.

Well-fired ceramic items were also available at that time, and by the middle of the nineteenth century mass-produced cast iron vases as well.

Ornaments had become a well established part of British landscape design during the seventeenth, eighteenth and nineteenth centuries – in part because patrons of the arts were influenced by their travels abroad, especially to Italy, France and Greece. The influx of sculpture and furniture from the Continent also helped to create a new awareness. Great garden designers of that time, such as Kent, Vanbrugh, 'Capability' Brown, and Repton, all knew the value of garden ornaments, though some of them swept away much of the formality of the past.

THE JAPANESE INFLUENCE

Japanese gardens make much use of the shape and form of inanimate objects, such as stones, pebbles and 'lanterns', even predominating over the plants, which become secondary to them.

During the twelfth century the Japanese garden, influenced by Zen Buddhism, became a dry landscape, with rocks and stones arranged on raked sand the main features. The garden was full of symbols – a place where spiritual values were promoted. Later, water (usually still and reflective) and more plants were introduced, together with ornaments and buildings.

One of the most frequently used ornaments in Japanese gardens was a votive lantern, offered to Shinto or Buddhist deities. The traditional lantern design has a low plinth, a pedestal, then the lantern housing, topped by a curved roof and a finial.

Japanese ornaments were originally symbolic, but they have become integrated into Western gardens for their purely aesthetic qualities, and the Japanese 'lantern' is now a popular garden ornament.

2

THE MODERN GARDEN

The great gardens of the past show how effectively garden ornaments and statuary can be used on the grand scale. They demonstrate principles and give inspiration. But it's easy to dismiss such examples of garden design as irrelevant for today. This is understandable if you've not seen for yourself how effective garden ornaments can be in a small garden. It can be difficult to transfer the mental image of great yew hedges and long avenues leading to an ornate fountain to a modern suburban garden, yet the principles – their use as focal points, their ability to bring interest to otherwise dull or uninteresting corners of the garden – are as valid whether you garden in a backyard or have boundless acres.

So why not cast aside preconceived notions and look afresh at how ornaments can be used in the garden? They can contribute to good garden design in almost as many ways as there are gardens.

THE REWARDS . . .

Statues and other garden ornaments have many uses, but they perhaps contribute most by acting as focal points, drawing the eye to a particular point and giving the garden a sense of direction. A path between two tall dark hedges may seem offputting and forbidding, but place a light-coloured ornament or bust at the end and you will feel invited to walk down it – you'll know there's a reason to explore. A small town garden that can all be seen at a glance will become more interesting if the eye is prevented from doing this by being focused on a tasteful statue or ornament at a suitable point. Using several in strategic positions will persuade the visitor to explore the garden, however small, section by section.

A garden can be plain and unadorned, just as a room can be sparsely furnished and decorated, or it can be well decorated with tasteful ornaments. It is not only the furniture that sets the 'tone' or mood of the home, but the ornaments and pictures used in it too. So in a garden the ornaments can set it apart from run-of-the-mill gardens and give it distinction. Figs. 1 and 2 show the transformation that can be achieved by adding a focal point to a mixed border, for instance. There is more to a garden than its plants.

Garden ornaments have other roles besides forming major focal points. Containers, for instance, can provide a setting for plants, or they can become part of

The ivies that frame this mask give it an almost humorous tone, but they need regular trimming.

Figs. 1. and **2.** Without a bust, this shrub border would look fairly ordinary, but providing a focal point gives it a sense of purpose. At ground level the bust seems out of proportion and almost insignificant but brought to eye level with a pedestal it immediately commands attention.

a plant grouping. Plants that surround or accompany large ornaments might seem insignificant, but small figures placed among plants will actually draw attention to them. This can be especially effective where bold foliage plants, such as hostas, are used.

Ornaments used as plant containers provide opportunities for creative planting and enable you to introduce variety into an otherwise static feature. In a setting in an open part of the garden, where cool and tranquil statuary would be out of keeping, a tastefully planted urn could make an 'architectural' contribution and provide the necessary warmth and colour to act as a focal point.

Statues, vases, and urns can be used to arrest the eye on a sloping grass bank that would otherwise be disturbing, or to relieve the monotony of a long hedge by breaking up the horizontals. All ornaments, however humble or grand, provide emphasis and accent in a garden. They draw the eye, demand attention. In their stillness they also contrast with the living plants around them.

THE PROBLEMS . . .

If you get the scale or the materials wrong, your focal point will simply draw attention to an error. No matter what the ornament is, whether cheap or expensive, its success depends more on getting its position right than its artistic merit or the material it is made from. Remember too that ornaments can be overdone. Too many will fight for attention and instead of taking the eye to a particular point will confuse it with their competing demands. Unless you are creating a formal garden – perhaps with bays, each holding a suitable figure, or an avenue in a long garden with ornaments coaxing the eye along it – avoid having more than one or at most two in view from any one vantage point. If you've followed the rules of good design, and created divisions – 'compartments' or 'rooms' within the garden which prevent it all being seen at a glance – this shouldn't be difficult.

If you overdo the statues in a small garden, it will assume the atmosphere of a cemetery.

Also take care when using ornaments as plant containers. If you overfill them with garish flowers these will detract from the ornament and you might as well use some cheap plastic container. You need to ensure that your choice of plants and containers are complementary to each other (pages 36–40).

AND THE CHALLENGE . . .

Ornaments should never look as if they've been added. To look right they should seem to belong there. This is why you must find the right ornament for a particular spot, rather than trying to find a niche for one you happen to like.

In later chapters examples of ornaments and statues used in a variety of settings are described, but you may think of many more. Provided your garden is *planned*, and they are deliberately used as focal points, there are plenty of places you can use them effectively. Might a light-coloured statue bring interest to a dark corner of the garden where it's difficult to grow colourful flowers well? Could a plain wall be transformed by a gargoyle or mask with a small water spout? Would a small ornament set among hostas help to sustain interest during those long months when their season of beauty is over? Would a sundial or birdbath transform a rather uninteresting lawn? Could the entrance to your drive be improved by finials on the gate posts? Have you thought about using natural 'sculpture', such as large boulders, in a flower bed? Or would your conservatory look more distinguished with the right figure surrounded by a skilful planting of evergreens and flowering plants? Forget the rampant lions or plaster spotted dalmatians perched over the porch if you live in a modest suburban house. It's not difficult to find many more suitable statues and ornaments if you use your imagination.

A wild area of garden like this could be very dull. The statue has transformed it into a tasteful retreat.

Statues and ornaments can be especially useful for punctuating a cool, shady border with lots of greens.

Using garden ornaments wisely is always a matter of balance: getting the proportions right, not using too many ornaments, yet having the vision to think big when necessary. There are many conflicts – deciding whether to spend your money on a couple of different ornaments for separate parts of the garden, or to invest in a pair of identical ornaments to use as a matching pair. The latter course is often difficult because it can make the purchase expensive, but it could be the better choice. A pair of finials, vases, or urns can dramatically transform a gateway or a flight of steps. They might even be used effectively to frame a vista.

Restraint is a challenge too. Having convinced yourself that a particular ornament will improve a certain view or enhance some group of plants, it's very tempting to rush ahead and put it there without looking at the alternatives – alternative pieces, which you'll probably have to visualize, or alternative positions for the same piece, which you might be able to try out. Train yourself to think how an ornament will look from more than one vantage point. Look at it from your house too – upstairs as well as down. This is especially important in a small garden where the various parts relate so closely, and where the whole of it can probably be viewed easily from the house.

Integrating the house and garden is another challenge. The suggestions made in this book presuppose that there won't be a clash of style with the house. If the garden's large you may still be able to indulge in different styles and moods, especially if it is divided into smaller areas with hedges, borders, or changes of level. But in a small garden the home will almost always be dominant. A Versailles tub by the back door, probably with a dustbin in the background, and pineapple finials at the gate, will hardly look right with a modern brick house on a housing estate. Many other ornaments will look less incongruous, and provided you never overlook the overall setting they should be successful.

Remember, garden design is concerned with more than a collection of good plants. It's also about the use of shape and form and textures. If you get the framework right and it looks good at all seasons, it will provide a setting that enhances the plants. Statues and garden ornaments should be an integral part of that design framework. Whatever the size or style of your garden, always ensure that the garden ornaments fit naturally into the overall design framework.

3

STATUES AND ORNAMENTS

No matter how clear the theory of using and siting garden ornaments might seem, it can be difficult to appreciate their potential in your own garden. You're used to seeing it the way it is, and this can make it difficult to envisage how it can be improved.

The best way to overcome this problem is to see how other gardeners have used ornaments successfully, then ask yourself whether something similar would work in your own garden. Provided you don't try to copy the idea too slavishly – no two gardens are the same – nor contrive to recreate something that is clearly out of character or style for your garden, this approach often works well.

Many of the illustrations in this book should provide ideas you could develop, whatever the size or style of your garden, and there are more ideas and suggestions in this chapter that should stimulate the creative use of garden ornaments.

There are dangers, of course. It's so easy to look at one corner or facet of a garden and see the potential of improving it with a suitable ornament, and then turn one's attention to another spot. The ornaments could then look as though they have been scattered around the garden as afterthoughts. Trying to bolster a poor design by using too many ornaments won't work. Use just a few to improve the dullest spots or to provide a focal point where the garden cries out for one, but don't go over the top. It might be better to think about a fundamentally new design. You want your ornaments to look integrated, as though they were planned with the garden, rather than as items peppered on to spice it up afterwards. The smaller the garden, the more obvious this becomes.

FIGURES AND ANIMALS

A suitable scale is vital if figures and animals are to look right. A pair of large rampant lions at the entrance to a small modern home could look pretentious – not to say ridiculous – and a large figure of a naked lady set on a small lawn is likely to dominate the garden and ruin any sense of design. A small lead figure or a reconstituted stone bust, tastefully sited, will probably set the tone far more effectively in a modest sized garden.

The quality of concrete or reconstituted stone ornaments can vary considerably, and this should also influence where you use them. Set among plants, or at

This genuine ancient statue is in a perfect setting, with a sympathetic background and plants to clothe the base.

Another very old piece from Italy, but a similar effect could be achieved with a modern reproduction plaque.

the far side of a pond, or at the back of a bed, the lack of fine detail probably won't matter. The overall shape is what's important. But if you are setting a bust in an alcove in a wall, or placing a statue on a lawn or by a path, it will be closely inspected, so you do need something that will stand close scrutiny.

BUSTS are especially versatile ornaments. A Roman god or satyr can look surprisingly at home in a modern setting. Some are quite small and would be suitable for a purpose-built alcove in a wall, or for setting on a plinth in the corner of a courtyard or patio. Large busts can give a touch of class to a formal garden if set on plinths against a dark hedge on one side of a lawn, or even in the corners of quite a simple garden formed only of lawns, hedges and evergreen shrubs. The simplicity of this type of garden often makes a better setting for busts than a colourful flower garden.

Don't overlook the possibility of using busts on low walls or retaining banks. Quite a large bust can be used without looking overpowering, as it might in a small area. Because it sits on a wall you can plant low shrubs in front of it, and even let plants scramble up around it. If it's a retaining wall it should also be possible to use plants behind and around it. With skilful planning and planting, such a bust can be framed by plants to make a real feature out of what would otherwise be a rather uninteresting bank or retaining wall.

COMPLETE FIGURES are more difficult to position tastefully, especially large ones. Pale-coloured statues, usually of reconstituted stone, are always conspicuous – and if they are large as well they will be dominant. They can, of course, be striking and attractive for that very reason. They are particularly effective if you exploit this dominance by setting them with *low* shrubs in front of them at the back of a shrub border, that would otherwise lack year-round interest; at the far side of a fairly large pond, with shrubs behind; or simply part way along a long, dark evergreen hedge to act as a punctuation point. An ornament of this kind could equally well be used beneath a tree with a suitably tall, light canopy. Juxtaposed with a white-barked birch, against a dark background, the effect can be stunning. But it's generally best to avoid siting this kind of statue in a prominent *central* position.

Small figures are more easily placed. Set on a pedestal, one would provide a striking focal point in an otherwise dull corner of a patio or courtyard. They can also look superb in a formal setting, perhaps by a flight of steps with dark evergreens behind, especially if the figure is illuminated for part of the day by shafts of sunlight filtering through surrounding trees.

Generally, the smaller the figure, the more important the planting around it becomes, especially if a plinth or pedestal is used. A small figure on an exposed plinth can look unplanned, but if you plant attractive flowering or foliage plants around the base, partly hiding the plinth or pedestal base, the figure will be transformed, looking integrated and intentional.

Figures can also be used in flower beds, even if the plants are mainly herbaceous, but the figure's colour and style have to be right. A traditional French-style figure in a terracotta colour, perhaps 1.2–1.5 m (4–5 ft) high, will mellow with age and look really good in summer with the plants growing around it, yet it won't appear stark in winter when there's less plant growth. Figures of this kind also succeed in a cottage garden setting, as they have a more mellow, rural appearance.

Small figures are often successful used in pairs, but can be more interesting if the pair clearly belong together without looking identical. Try flanking the sides of a flight of steps, a gateway, or even the door to a potting shed or outbuilding, with a pair of small figures, and you will see then what would otherwise be an unexceptional feature assume a new importance. Here too it will help to soften the appearance of any pedestal or plinth with plants.

ANIMAL ORNAMENTS can say a lot about the gardener's interest in pets. Having large figures of dalmatians in the front garden is more likely to indicate an interest in these dogs than in good garden design. Not that there isn't a role for animal ornaments, but you need to be aware of the problems. A pair of eagles used as gate post finials will probably suggest nothing but good taste; a stag on a broad plinth used as a focal point against trees in a large garden; or a greyhound flanking a raised daïs but cleverly integrated with plants, can also be perfectly acceptable. Herons and frogs make fitting ornaments to place by a water garden (see page 53), but if you just set them on a small front lawn they will look like garden gnomes.

URNS AND VASES

Urns and vases – urns being vases with a top or lid – fulfil similar roles, but vases need to be planted if they are not to look incomplete.

Vases and urns are difficult to place convincingly in a small or modern garden. They fit more comfortably

Fig. 3 If you've bought an expensive vase or container, choose plants that have a strong outline but won't detract from the detail on the ornament itself.

Fig. 4. Attractive though this type of planting can be, with too much colour and cascading plants, the container itself can become a secondary feature.

in a garden that has balustrading, or where they can be used as focal points at the end of a long walk or drive. Used as a centrepiece they can also give a sense of purpose to a large formal garden.

Urns don't have to sit on plinths. They can be equally successful capping a low wall, or punctuating a terrace where there's a change of level. But be careful not to set a large urn, even on a plinth, where it could look more like a gravehead monument than a garden ornament.

Vases are easier to accommodate than urns because they can serve as flower containers as well as being ornaments in their own right. Some very decorative vases and containers may be best without plants. In a suitable setting they display a classical dignity that would be ruined by plants.

It's important not to over-plant any decorative vase or its beauty will be diminished. Go for fairly upright plants, or choose those with a strong, distinctive shape (see page 40), rather than very colourful plants or trailers that will hide the shape or detail of the container (Figs. 3 and 4).

JARDINIÈRES, TROUGHS AND TUBS

A jardinière needs a distinctive plant that will reflect the strength of its design rather than compete with it. Try a *Fatsia japonica*, a yucca, phormium, or even a hydrangea or camellia, rather than a miscellany of flowering plants. Keep massed colourful annuals for cheaper troughs and hanging baskets, and use choice shrubs with a simple outline that will not detract from the ornament.

Decorative troughs are available in a wide range of shapes and sizes, in terracotta as well as reconstituted stone and other materials, including glass-fibre and glass-reinforced concrete. Some of the more substantial ones look good raised on pillars or plinths, but the vast majority are used at ground level.

Unfortunately it's often difficult to see the detail on them, especially if large or cascading plants are used. If you can use them on a daïs or even a low wall, they are less likely to be overlooked, and the plants can probably be better appreciated too. It pays to use small, compact, upright plants, such as pansies or primroses, that won't hide the decorated sides. If you want something bushier and more cascading, small, arching varieties of fuchsia would be suitable as they give good, bushy cover yet leave the sides visible.

It may seem wrong to suggest using wooden tubs, given their probably short life compared with the more durable materials discussed so far. Most wooden containers are naturally considered primarily as plant containers rather than garden ornaments. But the traditional Versailles tub, and variations on it, have the same design potential as jardinières, with the advantage that they blend in more satisfactorily with painted wooden seats. White-painted Versailles tubs look superb against a dark hedge or flanking a white-painted timber seat in a bay set into a hedge or border.

If the garden has been designed to a classical theme, use shrubs such as sweet bay (*Laurus nobilis*), but for a more modern style choose a mass of agapanthus, crinums, or phormiums – any plant with a strong outline and a bold appearance. But try to keep to just one kind for maximum impact.

PLAQUES AND MASKS

Wall plaques are suitable for most gardens, provided you choose a suitable style. Those of reconstituted stone, terracotta and ceramic all have a different 'feel' and each creates a different kind of mood. Concrete or reconstituted stone plaques generally look best where they reflect the material and style of other ornaments in the garden. Try using this kind of plaque on a wall where steps turn a corner, or anywhere that a visitor would otherwise be faced with a plain or uninviting expanse of blank wall.

Finials can make much more of a focal point of a gateway or a flight of steps.

A terracotta or colourful ceramic plaque, or a stone or concrete mask, could be more in character in a courtyard or patio setting. If you want to make it more of a focal point, a wall mask with water spout will certainly attract attention.

In a cottage garden, or in a courtyard, a colourful ceramic plaque, or a subtle terracotta one, will make a focal point that doesn't look out of character.

a

SUNDIALS

You can buy a surprising range of sundials, from some very pretty antique style dials to really modern wall-mounted designs. From the garden design viewpoint it's probably best to confine the choice to the pedestal or free-standing type. If you are considering a wall-mounted sundial, bear in mind that the wall needs to be sunny, then ask yourself whether a colourful plaque might not be more effective the year round. But this would not hold true for a period house, where it would add character to the building as well as the garden.

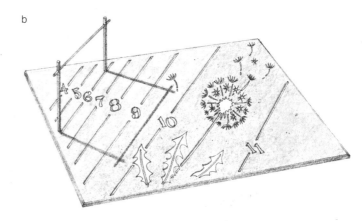

b

A sundial is one of the few ornaments that make a good centrepiece to a formal garden (a sundial was often the centrepiece of an old knot garden or parterre) or even for the lawn of a modern, more open style of garden. In a lawn it will look better standing on a small paved area, or some other kind of base, such as gravel, set into the lawn, rather than its pedestal rising directly from the grass, when it could look unbalanced and make mowing round it more difficult.

Two distinct elements need to be considered with a sundial: the plinth and the dial – each affects the tone and image that the sundial creates. The pedestal can be ornate and 'period' in character, or plain and modern – perhaps even ornamental walling blocks if they fit

c

Fig. 5. Even the traditional sundial (*a*) can have an attractively designed face, but you can also buy some striking modern designs from specialists (*b*) & (*c*).

the image of a modern patio. Choose one that corresponds with the style of the garden and with the other ornaments in it. If you choose a very ornate or old-fashioned pedestal for a modern setting, it will almost certainly look wrong. Be prepared to shop around for one that looks right – you can always buy the dial separately from another supplier if necessary.

While the pedestal will contribute most to the sundial's role as a focal point, the dial will give it character and interest on closer inspection – and a sundial invites close scrutiny in a way no other garden ornament does. Dials are made from many materials, including bronze, brass, stainless steel, and stone, including slates. They are as diverse as the artists who create them (Fig. 5). You could even commission a unique design to suit your individual tastes and requirements.

Don't assume that all pedestal sundials have a gnomon that casts a shadow on a conventional flat base. An armillary sphere (Fig. 6), which will make a powerful focal point anywhere in the garden, provided it's in a sufficiently sunny place, has connecting rings or bands, the more complex ones giving details of things like the meridian, as well as the hour. And for something really stunning in a modern setting, you could buy a stone globe dial mounted on a stainless steel column. The time is read off where the sunlit surface meets the shaded part of the globe.

The dial has to be positioned carefully if the reading is to be reasonably accurate. Advice on this is given on pages 72–3.

. . . AND BIRDBATHS

Birdbaths can be used anywhere that a sundial is appropriate, but there are many additional opportunities. Rather than site one in the centre of a lawn, put your birdbath towards one end, perhaps in a bay of a sweeping informal lawn, or near the house so that you can watch the birds using it.

Fig. 6. An armillary sphere (with rings for the meridian and the equator), is more striking than a normal sundial.

This kind of ornament, useful for a cottage garden, needs to blend in with careful planting.

This sundial is the centrepiece for a timeless gravel garden that could be in town or country.

PIER CAPS AND FINIALS

The pier caps and finials most of us are familiar with are the balls and 'pineapple' finials at the entrance gates to large drives, but small ones can be equally decorative on a strongly built garden wall. There are often opportunities to use them *within* the garden. A garden divided into sections is almost invariably more interesting than one that can be taken in at a glance. Internal gates can be a very effective feature, and if strong pillars are used can be made much more imposing with suitable finials. A falcon or eagle finial could be very imposing here, as well as decorative.

OBELISKS

If you associate obelisks only with monuments perched high on distant hillsides, you'll certainly be missing opportunities in your garden.

You need the right setting for an obelisk to be worth considering, but given a fairly large garden with a long lawn flanked by flower beds and a hedge at the end, a simple white obelisk could be just the kind of punctuation point that suits the style of your garden.

Even in quite modest gardens, a couple of small obelisks flanking a path where it disappears through an opening in a tall, dark yew hedge, can take the eye to it and make a feature of what would otherwise look little more than a gap in the hedge.

Erection needs almost as much care as the siting, and is something on which you need the advice of the manufacturer – if possible get them to erect it for you. You need a good, solid, absolutely level foundation, and fixing the upper sections of a tall obelisk needs suitable equipment.

Of all the ornaments mentioned in this book, though, obelisks are perhaps the most difficult to place in a small modern garden. They can so easily look pretentious. Don't dismiss them, but think carefully about alternative ornaments first.

ABSTRACT OR ADVENTUROUS

You need a strong sense of design and plenty of imagination to use abstract or 'modern' sculptures and ornaments successfully in a garden. Some can be tremendously successful with their strong visual images, but you need confidence to risk some of them in an 'ordinary' garden. Generally, the whole garden ought to have a strong and sympathetic design if such pieces are not to look incongruous.

Bold pieces can be very successful though, if the garden can take them. You could make a small masterpiece out of an old chaise-longue and a load of broken crockery, perhaps set on a lawn, with a green hedge as a background, that would give a dull corner a sense of vitality that has to be seen to be appreciated. Pieces of metal, or combinations of materials in abstract shapes can assume a 'presence' that is difficult to ignore. The images created can be just as strong as those from a lifelike sculpture. You may be able to buy these works from contemporary artists, or commision them, or even have a go yourself if you feel that you can express yourself that way. But be bold – it's no use half-hiding them. Find a setting that suits the piece, and make it a real focal point.

Bear in mind that the attraction of statuary is its shape and how it relates to its surroundings. Modern works can have as much relevance for us, possibly more, than a mythical god, and if you can ignore traditions and judge a piece purely on its merits, you may be highly pleased with an abstract ornament. Maybe it has more tactile qualities, perhaps it includes the sight or sound of water, it may simply be more intriguing than a classical figure or ornament.

Some of the illustrations in this chapter show how visually powerful some abstract works can be, and for the artistically attuned these will probably have a strong appeal. But don't expect the more extreme pieces to look right in a plantsman's garden. They are most likely to work successfully where the plants are treated along with the ornament or sculpture as paints on the creative palette.

USING PLANTS

It may seem odd to think of plants as enhancing an ornament, when ornaments are intended to enhance the garden. But the right choice of plants will help to integrate the two elements. It's impossible to suggest more than a few planting ideas, as almost endless plants and combinations of them could be used. But once you can see *how* different types of plants can be used, other candidates will suggest themselves to you.

Plants as backdrops

A white statue or a bust on a pedestal is likely to be most striking if its background is clean, uncluttered, and dark enough for the ornament to stand out against it. A dark, evergreen hedge is ideal. Yew (*Taxus baccata*) is one of the best, but even common privet (*Ligustrum ovalifolium*) can be effective.

If you have a boundary wall instead of a hedge, a similar summer effect can be achieved by using a vigorous climber such as Virginia creeper (*Parthenocissus quinquefolia*) or Boston ivy (*P. tricuspidata*). They are deciduous so you will have a bare wall as a background in winter, but the changing seasonal pattern can give different perspectives on the ornament, and these plants give a brief but glorious display of autumn reds that can bathe a statue in a warmth it lacks at other times.

Vitis coignetiae is another deciduous climber that will give a final fling of autumn glory before its large leaves, occasionally 30 cm (1 ft) across, drop and leave the wall bare for winter. This is a vigorous climber suitable for covering an outbuilding, with some shoots cascading to frame a suitable ornament.

Bamboos too can make an interesting yet unobtrusive background for statues.

Within the garden, on a patio say, a trellis covered with a honeysuckle like *Lonicera japonica* and its varieties such as 'Halliana', or *L. × americana*, will make a pretty curtain in leaf or flower against which to view.

Ivies, whether covering a trellis or a wall, are also suitable, but choose a small-leaved kind or one of the plain green large-leaved forms such as *Hedera colchica* (avoid variegated large-leaved varieties, which can detract from the ornament). You can even allow a small-leaved ivy to scramble up and around an ornament provided you trim it back if it threatens to become too rampant.

Hiding the base

Plinths and pedestals can be very decorative but will look even better if the base, and perhaps the foundation, is camouflaged and softened by suitable plants. Evergreen groundcover plants are probably best. Bergenias with large rounded leaves, which often turn reddish in winter, have a strong, positive shape and contrast well with a white plinth. *Calluna vulgaris* varieties (heathers) are worth considering if you can plant them in a broad sweep, and *Gaultheria procumbens* is a super plant to use if you can give it a peaty, acid soil.

Drifts of epimediums can provide year-round cover without competing too strongly for attention. For bold winter colour and useful summer interest, try planting *Euonymus fortunei* varieties such as 'Emerald 'n' Gold' or 'Emerald Gaiety'. *Lamium galeobdolon* 'Variegatum' (syn. *Galeobdolon luteum*) is a spreader, not so good for the base of a rectangular plinth, but useful for masking the base of a large reconstituted stone animal, for example.

For carpeting the soil round ornaments, some of the cotoneasters can be very attractive. *C. dammeri* is a ground-hugging plant, specially interesting in autumn when its shoots are studded with red berries. If you want a cotoneaster that will also grow upwards to hide the plinth, the ever-popular *C. horizontalis* deserves your consideration.

Don't overlook deciduous plants. They provide no

An armillary sphere (a kind of sundial), used as a centrepiece and focal point of a formal herb garden.

A very simple sundial, but nevertheless highly effective as a focal point because of its position.

cover in winter, of course, but some have such a strong or interesting outline that it's worth accepting that drawback. Hostas come in such a variety of leaf shapes, sizes and markings, that there are bound to be some varieties you could use. Lady's mantle (*Alchemilla mollis*), with soft grey-green leaves that glisten with the moisture they capture and hold after rain or dew and pretty almost fluffy sprays of yellow-green flowers, makes a useful base cover for almost any ornament.

Scramblers and climbers

Some weak-growing climbers can be used very effectively to climb and hang on to a large ornament, such as an urn on a low gate-post, or a large ornament on a pedestal. Try the daintier clematis, like *C. alpina* and its varieties, or *C. macropetala*.

More vigorous climbers can be used to clothe tall pillars if you are prepared to tie them initially. Hops (*Humulus lupulus*) can be used for this, and the large-leaved vine *Vitis coignetiae* is suitable if the pillar is large – and good for a pergola too.

You need to plant climbers in scale with the structure. Climbing roses for instance, can be pretty on a light timber pergola but look quite inadequate on a large one. Choose bold, vigorous plants for a pergola built with brick or reconstituted stone pillars. You could use grape vines, but *Vitis coignetiae* has much bolder foliage, and a wisteria is infinitely more striking in flower.

Frame it with shrubs

It's sometimes a good idea to surround an ornament with plants, so it is the centrepiece in a living frame. The choice of shrub must depend on the size of the ornament and its height from the ground, but a mixture of cotoneasters, grey-leaved shrubs like *Senecio* 'Sunshine', and bold plants like hydrangeas, could be used. Sometimes contrasting shapes and colours can look more 'artistic' than a simple frame of plain evergreen shrubs.

Statues in flower beds

Statues can be used very effectively in mixed borders, surrounded by herbaceous and shrubby plants. The important consideration is height – the statue should not be so high that it towers above the plants, nor should it be dwarfed by them. Usually a statue about 1–1.2 m (3–4 ft) high is about right, but be guided by the plants used.

A statue can also blend in well with herbs. It could form the centrepiece of a herb garden, or simply merge into feathery fennel or emerge from sages and thymes.

Planting in containers

You could, of course, fill vases, jardinières and other ornamental containers with summer bedding plants. This might be the best solution for some low troughs, replanting with spring-flowering bulbs and plants in autumn. But for larger containers most bedding plants are too small and low-growing, so they look out of proportion. They can also look rather garish and out of harmony with pieces of classic design. It's better to consider some of the alternatives.

Jardinières and other large containers that provide a good depth of compost are ideal for shrubs, many of which would be unsuitable for more modest-sized tubs. These will form permanent features so the containers never look empty. If you want variety, there is probably enough room in the larger jardinières to plant some seasonal bedding, or other plants that can be changed, around the edge.

Shrubs for tubs and jardinières

There are hundreds of good shrubs that will thrive in a large container, and the following is only a selection.

Aucuba japonica (spotted laurel) is an evergreen that will do well in sun or shade, in a large container or a small windowbox (if the plant is small enough). Consider one for a container in a shady, possibly cold, position, but choose a variegated variety such as 'Crotonifolia' – far more attractive than the plain green form. Its flowers are insignificant, but on a female plant there will probably be red berries ('Crotonifolia' is male, so try the female 'Variegata'). Aucuba is regarded primarily as a foliage shrub though.

Buxus sempervirens (box) is another tough plant, much associated with formal gardens of the past. If the container is small you could try the dwarf edging box *B. s.* 'Suffruticosa', but as this can look rather boring one of the larger variegated varieties, such as 'Aureovariegata' (yellow variegation) or 'Elegantissima' (white variegation), and in a larger container.

Camellias are among the very best flowering evergreens. Their glossy leaves are always handsome, and in spring their flowers can be spectacular. There are many varieties and hybrids to choose from, but as a starting point, consider *C. japonica* varieties such as 'Adolphe Audusson' and *C. × williamsii* 'Donation'.

Chamaerops humilis is a dwarf palm that seldom exceeds 1.5 m (5 ft). It's only likely to survive the winter outdoors in a mild district, so if you live elsewhere only use it if you can move the container into a conservatory for the coldest months. It is worth considering for a touch of distinction, perhaps in a Versailles tub or a large decorative terracotta pot.

Cordyline australis (cabbage tree, Torbay palm) is hardy in mild areas but won't be happy where there are prolonged severe frosts. As a young plant it looks rather like a yucca and will be happy in a large container, but it can eventually make a substantial trunk with the leaves high up, though by then it should have been discarded or planted in the open ground. 'Atropurpurea' is a purple-leaved form that looks especially good in a terracotta container.

Fatsia japonica is one of the best tub or jardinière shrubs. Its hand-shaped evergreen leaves and its distinctive outline make this an interesting plant at any time of year. Clusters of white, ball-shaped flowers may appear on mature plants in autumn.

Hydrangea macrophylla varieties are not suitable for small containers, but will make a bold show in a large jardinière in a partially shaded spot. You must be prepared to keep them well watered.

Laurus nobilis (sweet bay) can be damaged in a severe winter, but in reasonably mild areas it makes a good tub plant that can be left outdoors. It usually looks best as a clipped or trained specimen. (You can buy plants already trained if you don't want to take the time to do this yourself).

Nerium oleander (the oleander) is a Mediterranean plant that needs the protection of a greenhouse or conservatory in winter, so plant it in a Versailles tub or large container that you can move indoors for the winter. It could add an exotic touch to a terrace or patio when its usually pink flowers open.

Phormium tenax (New Zealand flax) is a splendid plant for a jardinière, with distinctive, spiky swordlike leaves. These plants need winter protection in very cold areas, but should not be harmed by moderate frosts. Phormiums are well worth considering if you want a plant of 'architectural' shape. There are dwarf varieties.

Rhododendrons are superb evergreens when in flower, and not unattractive when out of bloom. They need large containers but at least you can easily provide an acid compost if your garden soil happens to be alkaline. Avoid the very large varieties. The more compact *R. yakushimanum* hybrids are worth seeking out.

Trachycarpus fortunei (Chusan palm) is a tough palm, but will need protection in cold areas. It can

If you have a container like this old cistern, you can actually make it into a centrepiece.

This corner of a large lawn with large shrubs and tree behind would be rather gloomy without this interesting ornament.

eventually make a large plant, though growth is fairly slow in a container.

Yucca filamentosa never fails to attract attention when it's in flower, but its spiky evergreen leaves are a feature at all times. It's a tough plant that will survive in all but the coldest districts.

DON'T FORGET THE CONIFERS

Conifers can make rather uncompromising container plants. Many look rather stiff and poker-like. But some look perfectly acceptable in small concrete or reconstituted stone ornamental tubs, and those of upright habit don't detract from the beauty of their container. Among those worth considering for a start are *Chamaecyparis lawsoniana* 'Ellwoodii', *C. obtusa* 'Nana', *C. pisifera* 'Boulevard', *Juniperus communis* 'Compressa' (for a small container), *J. c.* 'Hibernica', and *Thuja occidentalis* 'Rheingold'. Choose an open position for all these. If planted close to a wall or hedge, the side nearest the wall will probably turn brown and the plant may develop a poor shape in time.

SOFTENING THE EDGE

In a large container there may be space for other plants around the rim, especially while the main plant is becoming established. You could fill this space with small bulbs or summer bedding plants, but evergreen perennials involve less work and ensure that the container looks well clothed at all times.

You could use small-leaved ivies, which will also cascade over the edge of the container, enhancing or detracting from its beauty, depending on its size, decoration, and the vigour of the ivy. Other popular evergreen plants for filling spaces are *Euonymus fortunei* 'Emerald Gaiety' (white variegation) and 'Emerald 'n' Gold' (gold variegation). They will cascade over the sides to some extent but never become obtrusive.

Hebes are also worth considering. *Hebe pinguifolia* 'Pagei' is a silver-grey carpeter, *H. × franciscana* 'Variegata' a compact evergreen with bright cream and green variegation.

PLANTS FOR VASES

Vases can be planted very successfully with bedding plants, with trailing lobelia and other such plants cascading over the rim, but some of the larger vases will look more striking with a single bold plant of positive outline.

A small *Cordyline australis* 'Atropurpurea', a single plant of the Mexican succulent *Agave americana* 'Marginata' (forming a bold rosette of spiky, variegated leaves), or a dwarf phormium can be very effective. All will have to be overwintered indoors except in the mildest areas. They will be more vulnerable in an exposed container than planted in the ground.

For something hardier consider some of the grey-leaved evergreens, which contrast well with terracotta but also look good in lead containers. Both shrubby and herbaceous types of artemisia are suitable provided you choose one that will grow in scale with the container. *Santolina chamaecyparissus* (cotton lavender) and *Senecio monroi* are other shrubs to consider. All will be enhanced by a few blending annuals in summer, such as pink petunias.

The large-flowered fuchsias are not hardy, so you'll have to overwinter them indoors or in a greenhouse, but the upright and semi-cascading varieties alike are wonderful summer urn plants.

Though you don't want to hide the beauty of any decoration, it's worth planting a few trailers, at least for the summer, if you want to make the plants as much a feature as the vase. One of the best, because it retains a good degree of horizontal growth and seems to blend with most other plants, is grey-leaved *Helichrysum petiolatum*. You can also buy a yellow-leaved form, 'Limelight'. Overwinter them in a greenhouse or garden frame. It's easy to take cuttings in the spring.

If you are looking for seasonal colour, and don't mind replanting, choose sturdy bedding plants that will stand up to wind and that tolerate dryness. Geraniums are one of the best for summer colour.

Fig. 7. Don't overlook the possibility of using lights to bring your garden to life at night. Try floodlighting or spotlighting an ornament. Even the shadows thrown can add a sense of drama, as this illustration shows. Use low lights, too, to cast a beam down towards the ground among low plants with striking foliage, or to illuminate a small ornament set among the plants.

Ornaments don't have to be large or elaborate to be effective. This owl adds a touch of warmth and humour.

This bust looks as though it *belongs*. Ornaments should never look as though they have simply been added.

Fig. 8. If a statue works well as a focal point during the day, it will probably be just as effective at night picked out with a spotlight. Fountains and ornaments in ponds also look good illuminated, and the fountains often split up the beams of light with movement. Low-voltage lighting systems are perfectly safe to use in the garden and even under water if they are designed for the job.

BACKDROPS AND SPOTLIGHTS

The use of plants as backdrops for statues and ornaments has been described on page 33, but there are other ways of displaying and highlighting ornaments to show them to best advantage.

A timber fence can be surprisingly pleasing as a backdrop, provided it has a strong design, perhaps with diagonal timbers, and is well maintained, with a dark shade of preservative. A washed-out, silvery fence that is beginning to disintegrate will simply detract from the value of the ornament. The brick walls of a courtyard or walled town garden can provide an effective setting for a wall mask or a bust on a pedestal, perhaps placed in one corner.

Take lighting into account too. Sometimes, perhaps at the end of a tree-lined vista, the natural light rays will only fall full on the figure for a few hours a day. This may make it ineffective for part of the day, though the way that the ornament is suddenly illuminated as if by a spotlight can be a very effective part of a changing scene. But you must be very careful over these spots. Take into account the angle of the winter sun, which may not reach the same areas as summer sun (or which may do so for a shorter time). You can of course use pale ornaments to lighten a dull corner that never receives any sun, but these usually work best at close range in an intimate sort of garden. Statues and ornaments to be viewed from a distance are best stood in good light, even though a dark background is often very effective.

Artificial light can be used at nightfall to bring a completely fresh dimension to the scene (Figs. 7 & 8). An ornament that is pleasant but unspectacular during the day can become dramatic once dusk falls and a spotlight illuminates it. A low-powered light positioned near the base may be all it needs if you simply want to illuminate an ornament against the dark background of a hedge or wall. But for figures set among plants, it's best to have a stronger spotlight that falls on the plants that surround and frame it. Statues and figures are generally much more effective with this treatment than say vases or urns. If you don't want to install a high-powered mains system, there are low-voltage garden lights that will be perfectly satisfactory for a small garden. These are usually run from a transformer located in the house. There is a surprising range of styles and fitting for both systems, and some of these are illustrated in Fig. 9.

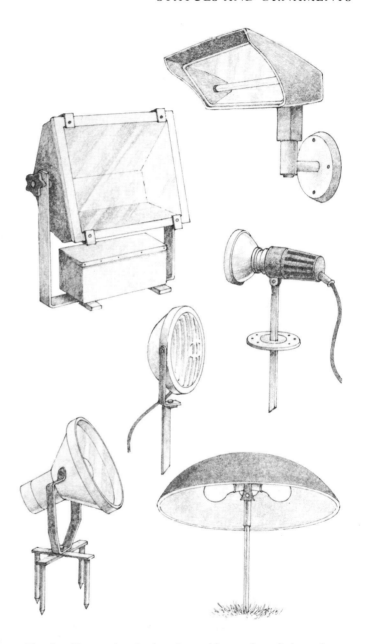

Fig. 9. You can buy both mains and low-voltage lights – these are just some of the types available. Try your garden centre or go to a good electrical shop.

4

FURNITURE AND DECORATIVE BUILDINGS

Not everyone believes that garden furniture should be conspicuous enough to form a garden ornament, but one need only look back at classic gardens of the last few hundred years in many parts of the world to see how furniture, and garden buildings too, have been used creatively. Seats in particular have a long tradition of decorative use, which can be traced back to the great Italian villas.

Furniture does not have to blend inconspicuously into the background, as some would prefer. Much garden furniture is purely functional, with no pretensions to good design, and relatively few pieces are intended as garden features. But by paying a little more you could probably acquire something that is useful *and* decorative.

If you simply want somewhere to sit for an occasional meal in the garden, a modern mass-produced patio set will probably be adequate, but good quality garden furniture of character can be decorative in its own right. Garden seats can form focal points as well as provide somewhere to sit. Victorian cast metal furniture can help create a period atmosphere, and a painted wooden seat has a timelessness that suits gardens old or new. But if furniture and containers are to be used creatively as

part of the garden design, they must either look antique or have a strong, modern design. But do avoid too much furniture if it's to have impact and not look cluttered. Too many chairs, especially, can look fussy.

SEATS AND BENCHES

It's a good idea to place a seat towards the end of a long walk or avenue. It gives the walk a sense of purpose, providing it with an objective. And, of course, there's the reward of a rest if the garden's long. It has to look inviting though, so a white-painted seat is more likely to be successful here than a timber seat treated with wood preservative. If you don't care for white-painted furniture, green can sometimes work well.

The trouble with white-painted seats is that they need to look pristine. Once the paintwork gets grubby the furniture looks shabby and uninviting – not the impression you want from something carefully placed for its visual impact. So you'll need to clean the paintwork regularly and repaint whenever necessary (see page 76).

If good design is uppermost in your mind, you may

A container like this adds a sense of purpose to what is already an interesting bordered path.

have to sacrifice comfort. Cast metal furniture can be fairly comfortable, but stone or marble bench seats will certainly not encourage you to linger long unless you carry a cushion with you. Yet they are among the most imposing seats you can have in a garden. They can look especially good on a terrace or near a balustrade. If you want a modern style choose one of plain, simple outline. For a more classical approach there are plenty of reconstituted stone bench seats with quite ornate supports. To fill a corner consider a curved bench seat.

There's no ideal position for sitting in the garden. In summer you'll probably want to sit in the shade, but in winter you'll be seeking the sun. If your seat is in the shade of trees or shrubs, you'll have to be careful that falling leaves and dripping branches don't become a problem. If you're using the seat as a garden feature, you should consider its visual impact above all else and choose the right material and design to suit the spot. Stained timber garden seats tend to be best in a sunny spot, white-painted furniture in shady areas. Cast metal furniture is not specially comfortable to sit on, but it may look the best in a garden that recreates a period style. You can always use cushions when you want to sit on it.

Don't be afraid to paint metal garden furniture if necessary. Wrought iron was always painted to protect it from rusting. Matt white looks elegant against a dark background. Black or even chocolate brown might be better against a light backdrop.

TABLES

The sort of tables you use for a garden picnic or barbecue are not likely to make good garden ornaments. The best tables for effect are those cast in reconstituted stone. But if you have stone bench-seats, it's probably not a good idea to put them with the table. You can hardly pull this kind of seat up to the table for comfort, and you'll almost certainly get better results if you use benches and tables separately so each

is shown off to advantage. When you want to use the table, it's easy enough to bring out a few light chairs for the occasion.

There are designs to suit a modern patio or an old courtyard, but all of them are substantial and need careful placing. They will look far more integrated in a small-scale setting if you have a stone vase in the centre containing flowers or a foliage plant. This prevents it looking bare when the table is not in use, and makes it much more decorative. You can always remove the vase when you want to use the table, but the chances are there will still be plenty of room around the vase.

RUSTIC SEATS

Rustic seats seldom create an impression of good taste unless in a natural setting, perhaps woodland. They are probably best avoided unless they give a sense of purpose to a woodland clearing, or can be integrated into an arbour or a shrubby retreat.

BALUSTRADING

Balustrading may not at first seem to qualify as a garden ornament, but it has been included because it represents something more than a mere wall or partition. It's decorative in its own right, and its classical connotations fit in well with that style of gardening that includes decorative urns and vases.

If the setting's right, balustrading can provide a superb transition between a patio or terrace and the rest of the garden. It is also a very acceptable way of screening off a swimming pool, especially if used with some attractively planted vases.

Many designs are available, and it's important to choose one that is in keeping with your house and garden if it is not to look pretentious. If traditional balustrading will not blend in, consider parapet screening – a compromise between balustrading and a low pierced (screen) block wall.

Balustrading is also useful for dividing a long, perhaps sloping site, creating strong lines across the garden and breaking it up into more distinct sections so there is more incentive to explore it. Terracing a sloping garden in this way, with gentle steps from one level to another, will provide plenty of interest, and the decorative walling or balustrading will add character. It also provides opportunities for incorporating ornaments – on parapet rails, especially at the top of a flight of steps, for instance. But don't overdo the ornaments, or they will fight with each other for attention, and impact and simplicity and purity of line will be lost.

TEMPLES AND PAVILIONS

These sound very grand, but you don't have to have acres of garden to do them justice. But you do need the right setting. Most temples and pavilions would look ridiculous in a small town garden, but if you have a garden in a rural setting, with a large lawn and perhaps trees or woodland in the background, rather than lots of formal flower beds or borders, this kind of feature could give your garden a touch of distinction. They are not cheap, however, so you need to be sure that the effect justifies the expense.

Temples are focal points to be viewed from a distance. In a large garden they fulfil a role that would be impossible for a smaller ornament such as a statue. They will take the eye even in the largest of gardens, where a simple ornament would go almost unnoticed. You could use an obelisk in a similar way, of course, but a temple is usually more appealing.

No matter how effective it might be from a distance, an empty temple can be extremely disappointing when approached from nearby. It needs some sense of purpose if it's to be worth approaching closely. A curved stone seat round one or two sides may be all that's required. This provides a reason for entering the temple. As impressive, perhaps more so, would be a central statue on a plinth. If the temple has seats, you could roof it with a dome, but if it's to be home for an elegant statue it will probably look better open to the sky.

You could incorporate a modern equivalent of a traditional pavilion in a small garden (even a fairly modest town garden) by choosing a smallish rectangular structure. You may find these described as garden houses, but don't expect something with enclosed walls. A pair, one at each side of the plot at one end of the garden with an expanse of formal paving and perhaps a long, rectangular pond to reflect the symmetry and formality of this style of garden, could look very striking.

A container like this placed in the centre of a lawn needs colourful flowers if it's not to look stark.

A large tree can dominate the garden, so why not turn it to advantage by making a feature of it?

PERGOLAS

The pergola is another import from Italy, where it was used primarily as a decorative support for vines. It is used to shade a path in those climes fortunate enough to get plenty of sun. It took longer for the pergola to be appreciated outside Italy than their statues, ornaments and fountains, and nowadays pergolas have generally degenerated into rather modest all-timber structures.

If used boldly, however, a pergola can be a striking ornamental feature. This usually involves building brick pillars or using reconstituted stone supports to take the timber beams. Timber uprights are perfectly satisfactory for a small pergola or one intended primarily to support climbers, but to make a real design feature of a pergola you need to think of something more substantial and permanent. The beams were traditionally made from oak or larch, which are expensive, but you could use other woods, perhaps cheaper softwoods, if these are more readily available. It is vital to use beams in proportion to the dimensions of the piers. You can, of course, buy reconstituted stone pergola coping to go with the piers. Pillars of this material can work out expensive and you may also need to allow for filling the hollow pillars with concrete and reinforcing rods. The beams may need similar treatment. This could be a job for a contractor, as even if you buy ready-mixed concrete, it still has to be delivered to the right level.

Nowadays pergolas are often attached to the house. The materials used must then reflect the building materials. But where you have scope to use a large pergola imaginatively, you are less restricted. You can use it to lead the eye to some distant part of the garden; to narrow or channel the field of view and perhaps screen off some less desirable aspect of the surroundings; or simply as a semi-covered walk from one part of the garden to another. But above all make sure it has a purpose – a large pergola stuck in the middle of a garden with no obvious purpose can look like a monument to bad planning. Make sure it leads from somewhere to somewhere – even if it's only to a statue or ornament at the end.

5

WATER FEATURES

Garden ornaments go particularly well with water. In some of our great gardens of the past, water itself was made a focal point. Fountains were built in most Renaissance gardens, and in gardens like Chatsworth in Derbyshire, England, were so powerful that their tall jets dominated the scene. Cascades tumbling down a slope are also found as focal points in many large European gardens and are a familiar feature of traditional Italian gardens.

Other designers chose to merge water and statuary more closely. Some of their creations might look almost grotesque to modern eyes but such focal points were relevant in their day.

In Japanese gardens, the role and affinity of water and ornaments is well known, and demonstrates more subtly how the two can be integrated even on a small scale in a modern garden.

The close association between water and garden statuary or ornaments is well established, but the two have to be integrated within the garden as well as with each other. Some ornaments sold by water garden suppliers may provide a bit of fun, but gnomes and figures fishing will not look right in a garden with a strong design element. Many of the popular fountains will add the *sound* of moving water, but lack the strong visual impact of a simple water spout or flow trickling out of an urn, or even a couple of plain small jets of water playing from each side of a small formal pool. If you want fancy jets, and you have the right setting, water bells or water spheres are like liquid sculpture.

ORNAMENTS TO USE NEAR WATER

It's a mistake to assume that water garden ornaments ought to be placed *in* the water or have water playing over them. A model heron placed strategically among waterside plants, facing towards the water rather than in it, can look particularly convincing. A stone figure placed at the far side of a pool, where its image is reflected across the surface, is pleasing too, and helps to give a pond a sense of purpose during the bleak months of winter. This is a good device to use where the pond has a background of evergreen shrubs or conifers. The figure will bring relief to the dark background and show up more effectively than against a more confused mixed planting.

White-painted cast metal furniture can add a touch of elegance to even a small patio.

By placing this white, elegant garden seat in a white border, it forms part of the overall design.

Pondside 'frogs' and other relevant animals can be successful nestling among the plants. Simply perched on the edge of the pool they can rank with over-decorated gnomes – fine if you fancy collecting them, but they detract from a sense of good garden design. These small pool-side animal figures are best used to provide an element of surprise, something to come across unexpectedly when you reach the pool. How well they work depends largely on how well you can integrate them.

Some figures – often animals but also griffins, a boy on a dolphin, or a Brussels boy – incorporate a simple water spout. These can be placed in the pool or by the edge. Much depends on scale. A small water-spout frog could look perfectly in proportion *in* a small artificial 'stream' or in a corner of a small informal pool, especially if surrounded with above-surface water plants such as water mint or marsh marigolds, but set in a large expanse of water or a formal setting, it could look trivial. Even water spouts set at the edge of the pool will look better with trailing plants around the base – creeping Jenny, *Lysimachia nummularia,* is undemanding and quick to grow – or surrounded by compact evergreens. Bear in mind that the pump will have to be turned off during the winter, so the figure ought to look equally satisfactory when the water's *not* running.

ORNAMENTS TO USE IN THE WATER

If you have a formal pool – rectangular or circular – especially in a part of the garden with formal flower beds but no trees or shrubs to give height, a fairly tall ornament in the middle of the pool could form a fulcrum for the whole design. It doesn't have to incorporate a fountain or water spout. If you want to make the most of the figure and its reflections, you need still water. But the figure will be so dominant that it must be tasteful with plenty of fine detail. If you're

also depending on the play of water, then cheaper figures with less well defined detail may be perfectly satisfactory.

In a less formal setting, selecting the best position is more difficult. Setting the ornament in the centre of an informal pool or setting can just look pretentious. It usually looks more effective offset to one side. Be guided by the setting – place it where you want the eye to be taken, or to bring interest to a dull corner of a large pool.

You may also need to consider the water plants when you decide on the best position, though it would be better to reposition the plants than compromise on the most pleasing position for the ornament. Waterlilies in particular do not like constantly disturbed water, so a water spout or fountain playing on them will probably spoil them.

Fountains or spouts set close to the edge of the pool can lose a lot of water if the spray is constantly blown on to the surrounding ground.

Ponds constantly lose water through evaporation in summer, too, so the level is never constant, even if you have a perfectly sealed pool. Don't set the base of the ornament so high that its plinth is exposed when the water level drops an inch or two. You can buy plinths designed to take a wide range of ornaments (Fig. 10), probably just over 30 cm (1 ft) deep, which is about right for most ponds. If yours is particularly deep or very shallow, however, you may have to build a firm and level plinth with blocks or bricks.

MOVING WATER

This book is primarily about using statues and ornaments, so ordinary fountains and geyser jets are beyond its scope, but water bells can be thought of as 'liquid sculpture'. A simple water bell produces a dome-shaped sheet of water between the top of the raised nozzle and the surface of the pond. Large bells with a diameter of about 60 cm (2 ft) need a powerful pump, but smaller versions, usually called bell fountains, operate with more modest pumps and can be screwed into many ornaments that normally provide an ordinary fountain spray. They can be arranged so that the bell envelops a small figure, which then appears enclosed in a sheet of water. Or a series of domes could be used on their own to provide a water display more in keeping with a modern formal garden than some of the traditional fountains.

SELF-CONTAINED WATER FEATURES

You can buy a wide range of ornaments that incorporate a self-contained water feature. Some are simple bubble fountains, perhaps rising from an artificial (glass-fibre) 'millstone', set in a surround of

Fig 10. Pond ornaments also need a firm base. It's important to have them at the right height, allowing for a slight drop of water level.

Imagine this picture without the Doric temple, then you'll realize how strikingly the ordinary can be transformed.

cobbles or beach stones. Others incorporate quite ornate statuary set on a plinth with the recirculating water cascading down into an integral dish. The latter can look pretentious in a small garden, but one could bring a paved area to life if the setting and scale are right. A millstone bubble fountain makes a superb focal point for a modern patio, and some of the more individually styled features, such as free-standing pedestal patio fountains, where the water falls back into a dish, immediately give a corner of some quite ordinary garden a touch of class.

Gargoyles or masks incorporating a small water spout can be used with a pool, but they can be at their most striking set into the wall of a small town or patio garden where there isn't room for a proper pool, but where the sight and sound of moving water is appreciated. It could also create a focal point in a small area where it would not be feasible to use large ornaments. Some have a small self-contained dish, but you could let the water cascade into a small sump, possibly covered or protected with large cobbles or beach stones. A small pump circulates the water, though you'll have to keep the water topped up in hot weather.

USING LIGHTS

Garden lights can be specially successful in and around a pond. Their beams are split and fragmented by a moving jet or reflected by still water. Low-voltage systems are available that make it safe to use lights even under water.

It's important not to overdo the lighting though. You can buy coloured filters to create all kinds of wonderful effects (some devices will change the colours automatically) but though these look spectacular they can look 'gimmicky' after a while. Underwater lighting can be disappointing too, especially as the lenses can become coated with algae which reduces the output of light. Quite simple spotlights can combine the dramatic with the tasteful. A beam that plays on to a fountain will sparkle beautifully, and a simple spotlight on an ornament can look really dramatic. Groups of waterside plants often look very pleasing illuminated in this way too, and if you use a light that can be moved around easily you can illuminate different groups as they reach their best.

THE JAPANESE EFFECT

The Japanese have traditionally used water symbolically in their gardens. In our gardens today we tend to borrow loosely from their style, taking their symbols but using them differently, without the underlying meaning that a true Japanese garden would have. It doesn't matter if we don't understand all the subtleties – it is a compliment that we find the Japanese style so aesthetically pleasing.

The essential elements of a Japanese garden are stone, rocks, sand, earth . . . and water. The use of plants is often restrained. The Japanese style will enable you to combine many different materials and shapes harmoniously even though they are assembled in a very unnatural way, usually with lanterns and other man-made symbols.

The principles involved in making a Japanese garden are beyond the scope of this book, but don't overlook these possibilities. Such a garden would enable you to use lots of strong visual images – water can trickle through a long hollow bamboo cane; you can incorporate an ornate bridge, perhaps painted red, over shallow water; or you can use stepping stones. And of course there is ample scope for ornaments. Keep to natural rocks if you have suitable pieces available of the right shape, or use lanterns in the shallow water or on the banks. A lead 'heron' and a stone Buddha would not look out of place in such a garden either.

6

PRACTICAL POINTS –
BUYING, FIXING AND REPAIRING

It's one thing to decide that garden ornaments are attractive or desirable, another to obtain them and fix them in position. Some are very costly, many are heavy or difficult to handle, a few potentially dangerous if not competently and securely fixed. This chapter is intended to help you through the buying decisions and to answer some of the questions you may have about fixing ornaments safely and securely.

WHERE TO BUY

Most garden centres have a reasonable selection of everyday ornaments, often made from concrete, though this may be painted and varnished to look very tasteful. Provided you want to use the ornament to provide shape and form among your plants, these are likely to be perfectly adequate for most gardens. But you may be able to get better quality ornaments at little more expense by going to specialist dealers or companies that produce illustrated catalogues, so don't buy the first that you see unless you're really convinced that it's what you want.

You may have to search further afield for the more expensive or unusual items, especially in reconstituted stone. It's probably worth visiting the show garden of one of the major manufacturers, where you can usually see the items in a garden setting. This will give you a much better idea of size and proportions than you'd get from mere photographs or dimensions in a catalogue. These show gardens will of necessity cram more ornaments into a small space than would ever be desirable in your own garden but you will probably come away with some useful ideas.

You may be able to take small items away with you, but larger ornaments may have to be made to order. Anyway they could be too large or heavy to cope with in a car, so you'll probably have to pay for carriage too. On heavy items this could be a substantial amount for a long distance.

If you have to place an order, remember to ask for an estimate of cost. And bear in mind that although garden centres should quote prices that include VAT (a tax added to the purchase price, levied in Britain and some other countries), prices quoted by manufacturers may not allow for this, so be sure to check.

Some companies specialize in antique garden furniture and ornaments, though these can be very expensive. If you can afford a genuine antique it's best to visit one of these to see what's available. They should also be able to look out for a particular item if you tell them what you want.

If you can't afford the genuine article, don't be snobbish about it – there are plenty of fine reproductions that few people would know from the real thing. Anyway, unless you collect antiques the most important consideration is whether it looks right, rather than its pedigree.

Antique dealers that handle a range of other items besides garden ornaments may be worth visiting, though some of them may stock plenty of imitations. You may get a bargain, you may not. Your best bet is to inform yourself of what prices are charged elsewhere, then you will have a means of deciding whether the price you are being asked to pay is fair or not.

If you want something unique to your garden, and can afford to pay for an individual creation, you could commission a contemporary artist or craftsman to create something for you. It's worth visiting art exhibitions to see if there's a particular style you fancy, then approach the artist. You could also try contacting art colleges for advice or contacts. Don't scoff at the work of young or newly established sculptors. The great sculptors of today and yesterday had to make a modest start at some time. If you do commission a work, be sure to provide a clear brief of what you're looking for, and where the piece is to be used.

You could compromise with something like a sundial by buying an off-the-shelf pedestal and commissioning a custom-made dial. But don't buy the pedestal until you have agreed on the style of the dial and gnomon, as the pedestal, dial and gnomon should

look as though they were designed as one entity.

You might also find someone who could paint a ceramic wall plaque for you. This could be a relatively inexpensive way of acquiring a unique, personalized ornament. If you have the right pedigree, you could even have reconstituted stone wall plaques made with your own coat of arms.

Distinctive rocks or boulders can make worthwhile focal points too. As particular rocks will be unique to your garden and should be relatively inexpensive to buy, perhaps even free, don't overlook the possibilities offered by a 'natural sculpture'. You might be able to obtain suitable rocks from a stone merchant, or from a quarry, or you may even be able to find a suitable one while you're on holiday – but don't remove rocks without asking the permission of the landowner. Anyway such rocks will have to be small if you are to get them home in your car. A local quarry should be able to supply stone that blends with the local landscape, and deliver it too.

Other fruitful hunting grounds include junk shops and jumble sales. Sometimes old everyday objects such as large earthenware jars can be useful. Try partially sinking one in the ground at an angle, filling it with cobbles or beach stones, or even gravel, with some of them flowing out on to the surrounding bed. A ceramic tile or plaque might be just what you need to add a touch of colour to an otherwise uninteresting wall. A small figure, perhaps carved from wood, could be worth buying if you can visualize it as a minor focal point, or can see it integrated with foliage plants. Such things needn't cost a lot, and keeping an eye open for the potential of the ordinary can be a lot of fun.

If you are looking for ornaments for a water feature or those traditionally associated with water gardens – Japanese lanterns, herons, and so on – visit a water garden specialist or send for some water gardening catalogues. You are likely to find a wider range of suitable ornaments than you would from companies stocking a more general range.

Wrought-iron furniture and lead statues are items often produced on a small scale by specialists. Your best way of finding them could be to look through

A striking 'temple' well integrated into the surrounded shrubs, and somewhere to rest after a swim.

This garden shelter is something that you might even be able to construct yourself.

the advertisements in gardening magazines, especially those aimed at the more serious and dedicated gardener.

MATERIALS – PROS AND CONS

Most of the cheaper ornaments are made from concrete, though the mixtures used and the resulting textures can vary from one manufacturer to another. The most expensive are likely to be worked from real stone. There are many other materials, though, traditional and modern, that are perfectly acceptable and often competitively priced. The following summaries will give you some idea what you can expect from the materials you are most likely to encounter, so you can decide whether they would be suitable. But in the final analysis a decision rests mainly on whether the particular piece suits a particular spot in your garden.

CERAMIC ornaments such as plaques can be quite inexpensive, though one-off items such as a unique sculpture or items in limited production can be costly. More than most other materials they can offer colour. Even a simple blue and white pattern can be very striking. All those intended for outdoor use should be frostproof, though they will be vulnerable to knocks or rough treatment. For that reason ceramic ornaments are best confined to areas where children are unlikely to damage them.

CONCRETE sounds completely unpromising, but it's strong and relatively cheap (though large ornaments can still be expensive). Compared with reconstituted stone, however, it can lack crispness of detail. How important this is will depend on where you are going to use it. Viewed at a distance it may not matter, but seen close to, a concrete seat, patio ornament or sundial may lack the necessary finish.

Some concrete ornaments are painted and varnished, perhaps red or green. They can be very striking and look more tasteful and expensive than their inner core suggests. Weight is a potential problem – large pieces are heavy and difficult to handle, and they need to be fixed firmly on a good base.

GLASS-REINFORCED PLASTIC (glass-fibre) isn't much used, but imitation lead troughs, for instance, look very convincing, are light to handle, and useful where weight could be a problem. You can expect years of trouble-free use, though the troughs are more liable to damage than lead, concrete, or reconstituted stone. Glass-fibre is also used with other materials – for the domed roof of a 'Doric temple', for instance.

GLASS-REINFORCED CEMENT can look like concrete or asbestos cement but has its own special qualities. It is mainly used for troughs and tubs, and has the advantage that it can be cast with a thinner profile than concrete. Strength is provided by glass fibres bound together with a cement mix, so it is possible to make troughs and tubs that are lighter and more elegant than would be possible with concrete alone.

IRON AND ITS SUBSTITUTES Cast iron is rust-resistant so it's suitable for year-round use in the garden, but aluminium alloys are used in modern castings. They lack the substantial appearance of cast iron. If you insist on the real thing you'll probably have to search them out at specialist dealers. Cast iron was often used for seat ends, with timber for the seat itself.

Although wrought iron used to be the local blacksmith's domain, there are still firms producing wrought iron garden furniture, though mild steel is sometimes used instead of iron. Steel must be well galvanized, and painted to prevent rusting. Wrought iron too should be painted to prevent rusting.

Nowadays reproduction iron or aluminium castings are usually protected with paint, synthetic enamel, or acrylic coating, when you buy them. Bear in mind that cast iron furniture with intricate mouldings collects dirt and is difficult to keep clean.

LEAD That great gardener Gertrude Jekyll, one of the most potent influences on twentieth-century English gardening, considered lead to be one of the best materials for garden ornaments in our British climate. It is still used for a few ornaments, but because it still involves a lot of hand craftsmanship it is generally expensive. Lead ornaments will be long lasting and trouble free however; they can last for several hundred years.

The subdued colour of lead and the delightful silver-grey patina it develops could be just what's needed for a spot where anything bold or bright would spoil the cool or tranquil effect. But lead doesn't have to be the colour of lead. It was often painted – white is popular, though you can use 'real life' colours – and if this helps make it a more telling focal point don't hesitate to try it.

Don't worry about lead poisoning or polluting a pond. Lead ornaments have been used for hundreds of years without ill effect. Once the surface has weathered there is little reaction from the lead.

RECONSTITUTED STONE is one of the finest materials for statues and garden ornaments such as urns, vases, and busts. Good ones are truly hard to distinguish from genuine stone and will last for generations – in fact they can weather better than some quarried stone, which can laminate and flake when weathered. Many are the (white) colour of Portland stone, but there are other shades, including the buffs of Cotswold stone, and even terracotta. It's simply a matter of adding dyes to the mixture. It may even be possible to get pieces made to match existing ornaments or buildings. The material is made from finely crushed stone mixed with cement, and probably an earth ochre to ensure the cement doesn't discolour the stone. The dough-like mortar is rammed into a mould by hand, then allowed to cure for a few days before being removed. After this, masons add the finishing touches. The stone is sometimes etched with hydrochloric acid to darken it slightly and give it a coarser, more natural finish. Some manufacturers offer an 'antique' finish for a small additional charge.

STONE clearly has a more individual value. Every piece has been hand carved (reconstituted stone is moulded, though it can be worked by hand after it is cast). Some soft stones can weather and lose their detail over the generations, but a piece you bought now would be unlikely to deteriorate much in your lifetime. If you simply want to use the ornament as a focal point, no purpose is served in paying extra for a real stone ornament, but if you want a collector's piece, you may consider it worth the investment.

TERRACOTTA quite simply looks natural and will therefore blend into almost any garden setting, traditional or modern. The sort of terracotta containers most likely to be used as garden ornaments are large decorative pots, wall masks, and perhaps ornate troughs (though the thickness of the clay required for troughs can make them very heavy to handle even when empty).

The biggest drawback to terracotta is that many of the ornate pots you can buy are not really frostproof but can flake or crack. If you buy direct from the pottery you should be able to find out whether they will withstand severe frost, but if you are buying from a garden centre or shop you have more of a problem. There's no simple way of being sure, but a pot with a very smooth finish – not to be confused with glazed pots – is unlikely to be sufficiently frostproof to use in the garden in Britain, or anywhere that they would be subjected to severe or prolonged frost. If the finish is rather rough, however, it will probably be frostproof.

Three things affect the frost-tolerance of terracotta: the firing (low-fired pottery is less likely to withstand prolonged freezing); the preparation of the clay, and the kind of clay used, though the latter is less important than the first two factors.

You can still buy hand-made terracotta ornaments, and you'll probably find they have a softer line than those produced by machine. Those made with very wet clay will have a pleasantly imprecise finish compared with a machine-made pot.

If you don't like the bright orange colour of newly fired clay, paint it with milk or yoghurt, and keep the

This small pool is the centrepiece of an integrated design where the plants and an ornament play an important role.

Always try to plant to enhance the ornament. Here the white *Calla palustris* makes an ideal companion.

ornament or pot moist. It will soon develop a patina of green mould.

WOOD isn't a popular choice as it is sure to rot or at least weather quite rapidly in a garden. But a nicely carved piece of wood could make a superb focal point among foliage plants, and it should last for some years – probably long enough for your needs. Wood is also widely used for garden seats and tubs. A white-painted Versailles tub can be a real feature.

Even softwoods have a respectably long life if you paint them regularly, but for choice go for teak, oak or iroko.

Western red cedar is very durable but unfortunately it lacks the strength of the hardwoods for use in furniture.

Whichever wood is used for garden furniture, make sure the dimensions are substantial – peferably at least 2 cm (¾ in) thick – at least 2.5 cm (1 in) for elm and softwoods.

WHAT ABOUT INSURANCE?

Insurance policies vary from company to company. What is likely to be covered can depend on where you live, so do check your policy. You might find that a garden gnome is covered against theft or damage, but the chances are that a valuable statue will be excluded from cover unless you've made special arrangements. If you have a very valuable garden ornament, or even a number of fairly inexpensive ones, it's worth checking with the insurance company. If cover is not included you can probably insure them for an additional premium.

If you fix heavy finials to gate posts or have mortared a bust to a plinth, it's worth making sure you have adequate personal liability cover. In some countries you may find that anyone injured as a result of your negligence has a claim against you if you have not provided firm foundations, say, or the mortaring or fixing was not adequately done.

Only you can know the likely risks and which of them you find it acceptable to take. But if you're aware of the potential problems you can seek suitable advice.

FIXING: DELIVERY AND ERECTION

Large ornaments may be delivered in several pieces, then assembled on site. It's best to arrange for the supplier to do this for you, if possible, as handling heavy stonework or concrete requires the right techniques as well as strong muscles and suitable equipment. Without such skill you could risk personal injury.

Some firms will assemble the various pieces on site provided no ground preparation is necessary. This is a useful service for larger items that can be very difficult to handle. However, you may be expected to provide assistance to off-load and erect the heavier pieces, though you will probably be telephoned first so that you can arrange any necessary help.

Pieces of more modest size – a bust or small urn to be fixed on to a pedestal, or a sundial – could be tackled by a competent handyman or woman on their own.

A large urn may comprise lid, bowl, and neck; a pedestal (probably hollow) is likely to come in three pieces – capital, shaft, and base. As the pieces are weighty it may be sufficient simply to place the pieces in position, but you can mortar them together – a good idea for peace of mind if there are children around, or if the ornament is in a public position, perhaps on a gate post.

FOUNDATIONS should reflect the weight they have to bear, but the following guidelines should help.

Ornaments placed on walls or a daïs or on balustrading should not create a problem if adequate wall foundations have been used. The ideal depth and width of a wall foundation depends on the type of ground and the loading. A strip footing twice the width of the wall should be adequate for a low garden wall, but make it three times the width if the wall is over 75 cm (2½ ft) high. The concrete footing should be at least 15 cm (6 in) thick, preferably deeper on clay soils that can shrink in dry weather. Provide a compacted hardcore base as well. If there are special problems, such as waterlogging, seek local expert advice.

If a deeper foundation is required, as where a structure is subject to Building Regulations (in Britain), or on shrinkable clay soil, a trench-fill technique may be required, but this normally requires professional equipment and help. It's not likely to be necessary for normal garden walls, but it's worth checking if the walls are connected with buildings. If you live in a part of the world where there are severe penetrating frosts, it's important to know the depth of the frost-line, as this should be taken into account. (If you live in the USA in an area where severe frosts are a problem, consult your local building department for advice.)

An ornament on a simple plinth presents less of a problem, though it's still important to provide an adequate foundation so the ornament is level and stable, and for safety reasons. Excavate an area about 15 cm (6 in) wider than the base of the plinth, and 45–60 cm (1½–2 ft) deep, ram a layer of hardcore into the base, and fill with concrete to just below the surrounding soil level. (If you are topping the foundation with paving slabs, allow for the thickness of these plus mortar if you are going to fix it permanently.) It's always worth asking the manufacturer what depth of foundations are necessary.

For most foundation work, a mix of 1 part cement to 2½ parts sharp sand and 3½ parts of aggregate is about right. You can use 5 parts of combined aggregate instead of aggregate and sand separately.

A pedestal or plinth being placed on paving slabs that are already firmly laid should be quite secure if bedded on mortar without further preparation.

To fix a feature permanently, a mortar mix of about 1 part masonry cement to 4 or 5 parts sand is generally adequate, but for copings and retaining walls with dense masonry use a strong mix of 1 part masonry cement to 2½–3½ parts of sand.

The exception to this is when fixing stone or reconstituted stone seats. (You will need to mortar the seat to the supports.) Although the seat will be strong it may be stressed and even crack if subject to pivoting or twisting strains. So use a weak mortar of 1 part cement to 8 parts of sand, then each support is more likely to bear an equal weight. As it will be weaker than the seat it will 'give' first, and if you want to resite the seat the mortar can be broken easily enough without doing any damage.

PLINTHS AND PEDESTALS

For some ornaments the manufacturer recommends a particular plinth, or it comes as an integrated unit, even if the parts arrive separately. But for others you have a wide choice of plinths or pedestals (Fig. 11). It's then vital to choose one that's in keeping with the ornament. A classical bust will probably look best on a Doric pedestal. For a decorative urn something plainer like a Georgian or Queen Anne pedestal or plinth might be preferable.

As an alternative to buying a ready-made plinth or pedestal, you could build your own from bricks (Fig. 12). This kind of plinth can be particularly effective in a cottage garden setting, or even for a modern sculpture. A surprising variety of moods can be achieved by using different bricks and by modifying the design. Red bricks will give a very different impression from the yellower bricks you can buy, and a straight column will give a different impression from one where the base is stepped out more broadly, with perhaps an extended row of bricks at the top before it is crowned with a paving slab. If the bricks overhang the main column, you may need to incorporate a sheet of stainless steel to help support them.

Whatever kind of plinth or pedestal you use, it must be level. Check frequently with a spirit-level, or use a plumb line.

If you're choosing a plinth or pedestal for a sundial,

This old urn fountain shows how effective the restrained use of water can be.

This small pond would look rather unexciting without the ornaments, but they've transformed it into a special feature.

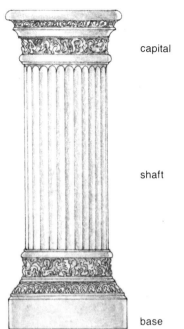

capital

shaft

base

Fig. 11 Plinths and pedestals usually come in three separate parts (base, shaft, and capital) to be assembled on site. Numerous designs are available, three of which are shown.

make sure it's not too high. The face should be low enough for the average person to read the dial easily.

To make an ornament look more imposing, you could pave an area around its plinth, flush with the grass. If you're fixing a birdbath, try setting it in a circular area of gravel to balance the dish on top of the pedestal. Such simple techniques can influence the apparent size and importance of the feature.

FIXING A SUNDIAL

When accurately set up, a sundial will show Apparent Solar Time (or Apparent Sun Time), which differs from Mean Solar Time or 'clock time' by an amount known as the Equation of Time. This is all to do with

the fact that the Earth's orbit around the sun is an ellipse. The practical implication is that a sundial can't tell our true time the year round. It will show a time about 14 minutes slow in February or 13 minutes fast in November (in Britain), and will be 'on time' for only a few days each year. An adjustment for Summer Time (where this applies) must also be made, though some dials have an extra scale that allows for this.

Most horizontal dial sundials have screw holes through which you can fix them to the pedestal. You'll need to use a masonry drill to make holes in the stone or brick, if these have not already been made, and use proprietary wall plugs to screw into. (Plugs and attaching instructions may be supplied with the sundial.)

Even if you want your sundial primarily as a garden ornament, it's still sensible to have it showing the time

Fig. 12. It's not difficult to make your own plinth from bricks topped with a paving slab, but remember to use frost-proof bricks.

as accurately as possible. That means orientating the slanting edge of the gnomon to point true north (not magnetic north), or true south if you live in the southern hemisphere. The gnomon should slope at an angle to the horizontal equal to that of the latitude at which you live. If you are buying from a distant part of the world you should check this carefully.

You can ascertain magnetic north with a compass,

then turn the dial by the magnetic variation applicable to your area. Alternatively you could synchronize it with a watch, but do so at noon (or an hour later if you have to allow for Summer Time). But to be accurate you should do this on or about April 16, June 14, September 2, or December 25.

Longitude also affects the calculation – and depending on the latitude the time shown could be consistently slow or fast throughout the year.

A good almanac should give you the 'equation of time'. The manufacturer should be able to advise if you have any other problems.

Some sundials come with a north-south-east-west orientation diagram for approximate positioning, but you will probably have to make further minor adjustments if you are looking for accuracy rather than mere decoration.

CREATING A WEATHERED EFFECT

New ornaments are sometimes rather stark until they have weathered. Within a year nature should have taken a hand and the growth of mosses, lichens, and even simple dirt, will have started to mellow the ornament. You may prefer to keep some ornaments – figures particularly – clean if you want them to show up well against a dark background, but generally weathering improves things. When new a bust will probably lack much of the detail when seen at a little distance and the main impression will be of the overall outline. Folds in a cloak and lines in the face are lost. But once time takes its course the bust will assume more character. Dirt, grime, even plant growth, tends to be more obvious on one aspect (depending on the prevailing wind and the direction of the sun for instance) and brings out the details in greater relief.

To speed up the colonization by algae and other forms of primitive plant growth, you could coat the ornament with something to provide an inviting surface for the spores to alight and germinate on. In the past cow dung and water would have been used, but nowadays any ordinary liquid fertilizer solution is more acceptable. Alternatively you could try brushing on milk or yoghurt to provide a sticky and nutritious surface which encourages spores to germinate.

Lead birds are popular as pond ornaments – they often blend in more harmoniously than stone ornaments.

If you have an ornamental heron, bear in mind that it can be as striking outside the water as in it.

REPAIRS AND MAINTENANCE

CLEANING ORNAMENTS

Though most of us want new ornaments to look weathered as quickly as possible, so they don't look so new and stark, it is sometimes necessary to clean one up.

It is not advisable to resort to drastic cleaning measures. A simple scrub with a hard-bristled brush and a mild detergent is usually sufficient to remove the worst grime. If stubborn stains or marks remain some diluted bleach could prove effective.

Terracotta pots sometimes acquire a white deposit. This is likely to be the result of salts leaching out of the compost as much as from the clay itself. In a garden setting this doesn't usually matter, but if you want to clean up the pot, try scrubbing it with a strong solution of vinegar.

Timber seats and ornaments will need regular treatment. Unless you want a natural finish to weather to a silvery-grey, treat them with a wood preservative before winter, but make sure the timber is still thoroughly dry. Don't use linseed oil, as it attracts dirt. If you want to smarten it up in the meantime, simply scrub the wood with soapy water.

It's a good idea to stand the feet of a seat in a can of preservative for 24 hours once a year when the wood's really dry, as these parts in contact with the ground are likely to rot first.

Clean away algae and dirt regularly from painted seats and tubs. Soap and water and a scrubbing brush may be enough, but you could try using wire wool on stubborn marks. Repaint the wood at least every second year.

If you plan to paint a lead ornament, use one of the older types of oil-based paints. Clean the lead by scrubbing it with soap and water first, but don't use a primer.

MAKING REPAIRS

A valuable ornament that has been damaged or has deteriorated through the effects of time may need professional attention. But there will be occasional small accidents to more everyday items that you can deal with yourself.

CONCRETE AND RECONSTITUTED STONE statues or ornaments are sometimes knocked or dropped, causing a piece of decoration to break off. These pieces can usually be stuck back quite satisfactorily with a two-part epoxy resin adhesive. It is essential to clean and dry the damaged pieces thoroughly first.

Making good damage when you don't have the broken piece to replace is not really a do-it-yourself job. But if you have a concrete ornament that needs patching up in a not very conspicuous place, you could try using a fine concrete mix then bond it to the ornament with a PVA adhesive such as Unibond.

Some manufacturers of reconstituted stone ornaments can provide a repair kit. You mix the preparation and apply it with a trowel or small knife.

The ornaments that you are most likely to need to repair are those of painted concrete. Small chips that would not be noticed on unpainted ornaments can be very conspicuous. Fortunately the job is quite easy once you obtain the right materials. The problem is matching the colour, but you should be able to buy small cans of special paint from a good supplier of ornaments of this kind. If you have bought the ornament there you should be able to obtain the matching colour (often a red or green). The same supplier will be able to provide a varnish, which is usually used to give it a glossier, better protected finish. When buying an ornament of this kind, it's worth asking whether touching up paint is available. A good supplier should be able to provide some.

LEAD ornaments can stand for centuries without coming to harm, but if you move them about it's possible that a limb of a figure may be knocked and damaged. Where mild steel was used for internal reinforcement in old lead ornaments, reactions can occur that eventually split the lead in places. Don't try to patch these up yourself, but get it done professionally. If you plan to have a professional restoration done later, don't try to patch it up with a glass-fibre repair kit, as this will make the final job lengthier and more expensive.

Although many small repair jobs can be tackled without any previous experience, clearly there are some jobs that need the attention of a craftsman, and we've indicated where this might be the case. The older and more valuable the ornament, the more important it is to seek professional advice if you are in any doubt at all.

If you are fortunate enough to have antiquarian stonework that is in bad need of repair, or even a matching pair of ornaments where one needs completely replacing, some of the companies given in the list of addresses on page 80 will probably be able to repair it or make a new one to match. Don't give up without seeking advice first.

INDEX

USEFUL ADDRESSES

Whenever possible it's best to see the ornament that you are buying, but it's also worth obtaining catalogues to see what's available. Most of the following British suppliers produce a catalogue (in some cases there may be a small charge), and you will probably find that the majority are used to dealing with export orders to the United States and elsewhere. You may find other local manufacturers or suppliers, so look through the gardening magazines too.

Brookbrae Ltd., 53 St Leonard's Road, London SW14 7NQ (01-876 4370). Sundials. Original creations made to order if you want.

Chilstone Garden Ornaments, Sprivers Estate, Horsmonden, Kent TN12 8DR (Brenchley 3553). A wide range of reconstituted stone ornaments.

Haddonstone Ltd., The Forge House, East Haddon, Northampton NN6 8DB. (Northampton 770711). A wide range of reconstituted stone ornaments.

Jim Keeling Flowerpots, Whichford Pottery, Whichford, Shipston-on-Stour, Warwickshire CV36 5PG (Shipston-on-Stour 84416). Clay pots and some ornaments, hand-made.

Minsterstone (Wharf Lane) Ltd., Ilminster, Somerset TA19 9AS. (Ilminster 2277). Reconstituted stone garden ornaments.

Renaissance Casting, 102 Arnold Avenue, Styvechale, Coventry CV3 5NE (Coventry 27275). Lead ornaments in traditional styles.

Stapeley Water Gardens Ltd., Stapeley, Nantwich, Cheshire CW5 7LH (Nantwich 623868). Large range of fountains, and statues and ornaments that associate well with water.

T. Crowther & Son Ltd., 282 North End Road, Fulham, London SW6 (01-385 1375). Dealers in antique garden statuary and ornaments.